FREE RESOURCES

to Deepen your Connection

Harvest Prayer Ministries, the parent ministry of *Prayer Connect* and PrayerShop Publishing, has multiple free helps that can encourage you in your daily prayer life. Here are some we invite you to check out:

Connection— a daily devotional on prayer that includes some inspirational thoughts and several Scripture-based prayer points. This can be emailed or RSS-fed to you each day. View it, or sign-up at **harvestprayer.com/connection**.

Scripture-Prayer— a daily passage of Scripture to read and then prayer points to pray about, using the passage. Designed to encourage you to practice praying Scripture regularly. It also can be emailed or RSS-fed to you each day. View it or sign up at **prayerconnect/blogs/scripture-prayer**.

Praye   t has a
section   subjects.
You are   ur prayer
times or   pture-based
prayer points or prayers. You will find them at **prayerconnect.net/resources/prayer-guides**.

HARVEST PRAYER
MINISTRIES *Websites:*

We encourage you to check out our ministry websites. Each has prayer resources that can help deepen your prayer connection with God or help you grow prayer in your church.

harvestprayer.com	**prayerleader.com**
prayerconnect.net	**prayershop.org**
prayertoday.org	**greatercalling.org**
40daysofprayer.net	**strategicpi.org**
ministrytoday.org	**prayerretreat.net**

 Like us on Facebook at facebook.com/harvestprayer, facebook.com/prayerconnect, or facebook.com/prayerretreat

DESPERATE *for* CHANGE

40 Days of Prayer for America

DAVID BUTTS

PRAYERSHOP PUBLISHING

TERRE HAUTE, INDIANA

Quantity Discounts Available
2 – 9 copies: 25% off; $4.50 each
10 – 24 copies: 33% off; $4.00 each
25 – 99 copies: 40% off; $3.60 each
100 – 999 copies: 50% off; $3.00 each
1,000+ plus copies: 60% off; $2.40 each

To order at these discounts go to www.prayershop.org.

For an additional $350, churches that purchase more than 2,500 copies can design their own cover and put their own introduction in the book. Call 812-238-5504 for details.

PrayerShop Publishing is the publishing arm of Harvest Prayer Ministries and the Church Prayer Leaders Network. Harvest Prayer Ministries exists to equip the local church to become a house of prayer for all nations, releasing God's power for revival and finishing the task of world evangelization. Its online prayer store, www.prayershop. org, has more than 600 prayer resources available for purchase.

ISBN: 978-1-935012-31-3

3 4 5 6 7 8 9 10 | 2015 2014 2013 2012

INTRODUCTION

P rayer is critical to any nation, especially a nation that proclaims a
connection to God. The United States historically had claimed
such a connection. But things have changed. We are living in
days that most call post-Christian. The drift from our Judeo-Christian
foundation is evident in almost every aspect of our society. That leads us
back to prayer. It's time to pray for America. This devotional is written
to help you focus your prayers in a biblical way.

Each day's devotion is based on a passage of Scripture. The Scriptures used here must be used carefully. Sometimes a promise was made
particularly to Israel as a theocracy (a nation whose leader was God).
Because of this, you cannot just pull any promise made to Israel and
automatically apply it to the United States or any other nation. But
many of these promises are based on spiritual principles that can be
carefully applied to our nation. I have attempted to do so, under the
leadership of the Holy Spirit.

I suggest you do not simply pray forty days and then lay this book
down and move on. There are several better ways to use this devotional.

One would be to pray this devotional through completely every
forty days. Imagine what could happen after a solid year of praying
these Scriptures and concepts over America?

Another way would be not to limit yourself to one devotion per
day. I believe the Spirit of God can take this material and forge powerful prayers for the transformation of a nation as we pray the same

Scripture day after day until the Lord turns us loose to move on to the next devotion.

The last devotion—Day Forty—focuses on Esther 4:14, in which the young Hebrew queen is challenged to put her life on the line for her people. Her cousin Mordecai saying to her, "Who knows but that you have come to royal position for such a time as this?" For such a time as this, we are all called to intense intercession for our nation.

DAY ONE

"The fear of the LORD is the beginning of knowledge, but fools despise wisdom and discipline." —Proverbs 1:7

This well-known passage of Scripture is typically used for individuals, and rightly so. The principle, however, can be applied to a whole nation. If a nation is characterized by the fear of the Lord in its dealings, both internally and internationally, it will be a nation known for wisdom and not foolishness.

A wise nation takes into account the Word of God as it makes laws. Even a cursory reading of the history of the founding of the United States demonstrates that our founding fathers seriously endeavored to base our nation's laws on their strong Judeo-Christian beliefs. Secularists today often counter that many of those men were, in fact, Deists, and not strong Christians. Their own beliefs aside, our Founders, almost to a man, insisted that laws were based on divine revelation and not on human wisdom alone. Even as strong a secularist as Thomas Jefferson said powerfully, "And can the liberties of a nation be thought secure when we have removed their only firm basis, a conviction in the minds of the people that these liberties are the gift of God? That they are not to be violated but with His wrath? Indeed I tremble for my country when I reflect that God is just: that His justice cannot sleep for ever." (Paul Leicester Ford, ed., *The Writings of Thomas Jefferson*, 10 vols., *Notes on the State of Virginia* (New York: G.P. Putnam's Sons, 1892-99), Query XVIII, 4:232.)

A significant shift has taken place in American political and cultural thought over the past fifty years, replacing God's Word as the source of morality, ethics, and law, with the rule of polls and surveys. This is exactly what Proverbs warns us against. A nation that rejects the Word of God as the basis for right and wrong has become a foolish nation that despises wisdom and rejects discipline.

Prayer Points

- Pray that the United States will repent of its corporate rejection of the Word of God as the basis of law.
- Pray that a holy fear of God will sweep across our nation, leading us back to a place of wisdom.
- Pray that courage born of wisdom will be given to Christians in places of leadership in government, the courts, and law schools across the nation so that they will stand for a godly basis for law.

My Prayer

Father, I give You thanks for the godly foundation of my nation. Thank You for instilling the fear of the Lord into our Founders, so that our laws were based on Your Word. Imperfect though they were, the original documents of government for the United States made a real effort to reflect Your will and Your truth.

Forgive us for drifting from Your ways. We have turned from the fear of God to the fear of man. Our laws change with the shifting winds of human opinion. We have embraced foolishness and rejected Your discipline.

We confess our desperate need for Your truth once again to become the foundation for our country. Pour out a hunger for truth and righteousness on everyone from preachers to professors to presidents. Raise up a standard of righteousness across this nation that honors Your Word and exalts Your name!

DAY TWO

"The LORD is a refuge for the oppressed, a stronghold in times of trouble." –Psalm 9:9

I f there was ever a nation that understood what it means to be a refuge for the oppressed, it ought to be the United States. The inscription from Emma Lazarus on the base of the Statue of Liberty has meant far more than words to millions. "Give me your tired, your poor, your huddled masses yearning to breathe free."

As a nation, by and large, comprised of immigrants and their descendants, many of whom were fleeing persecution or oppression in their own nations, we have been a land of refuge. The United States truly has been a stronghold in times of trouble for many.

Though this is a proud heritage and a significant part of who we are as a nation, we have always served as a refuge imperfectly. Some groups were more welcome than others. Some arrived and wondered if they were, in fact, better off here. We still struggle with what it means to open our national doors to others.

The good news is that the Lord is a perfect refuge, a perfect stronghold in times of trouble. He is a refuge, not only for individuals, but for a nation as well. When a nation turns to God, He will be a refuge for them. In the midst of the chaos of current events, whether it is financial collapse, terrorism, or war, how comforting to know that God wants to be a stronghold for our nation.

Prayer Points

• Ask the Lord to turn the hearts of the citizens and leaders of the United States to Himself.

- Invite the Lord to be your refuge and your stronghold.
- Pray that our nation will increasingly see that God is our only refuge in the midst of the troubles of this world.

My Prayer

Father, I am so grateful that You are my refuge and stronghold. I come to You today longing more and more to experience Your Presence and to rest in Who You are. Show me more of what it means for You to be my refuge in the midst of the storms of this life.

What I ask for myself, I also ask for my nation. Help us not to trust in our finances, our technology, or our military might. Lord, You are our refuge, our stronghold in times of trouble. We come running to You, Lord! Forgive us of our self-sufficient spirit. We need You, Lord.

DAY THREE

"This is what the LORD Almighty says: 'Administer true justice; show mercy and compassion to one another.'" –Zechariah 7:9

As a schoolboy in the late 1950s and early 1960s, I remember starting every school day by reciting the Pledge of Allegiance. The constant repetition allows the words of the Pledge to be recalled effortlessly today, half a century later.

"I pledge allegiance to the flag of the United States of America, and to the republic for which it stands, one nation under God, indivisible, with liberty and justice for all."

Have you considered the fact that a nation committed to justice for all is a nation that God can bless? God is passionate about justice because it is in accordance with His nature to be just in all His dealings. When nations base their laws and institutions on principles of justice for all, the God of justice is pleased.

Of course, this means that the contrary is true as well. When injustice creeps in, it brings with it the displeasure of God. God especially seems to look out for the welfare of those whom society overlooks . . . the poor, the less-privileged, the stranger, and the outcast. The nation that wants the blessing of God will ensure justice for all!

Prayer Points

• Thank the Lord that He is a God of justice and shows no favoritism.
• Thank God for a nation that proclaims itself a land of justice for all.
• Pray for our judicial system and lawmakers, that justice for all, tempered by mercy and compassion, will guide our nation.

My Prayer

I thank You, Lord, that You are perfectly just in all Your ways. You deal with us impartially, imparting justice while showing mercy and compassion. Help us to be like You in this way.

I'm grateful, Lord, that the United States has built justice into its very foundation. Forgive us when we have failed to carry out what we say we believe in. Help us as a nation to offer justice to all and not to discriminate in the way that justice is administered.

I pray for the judicial system of this nation. Restore godliness to the courts of our land. May those who make our laws do so with a deep commitment to justice for all. In the name of Jesus, we come against any spirit of privilege or special interests that would mar the true administration of justice. We cry out with the prophet Amos, "Let justice roll on like a river" (Amos 5:24). May a river of justice and righteousness sweep across our nation!

DAY FOUR

"Do not forsake wisdom, and she will protect you; love her, and she will watch over you." –Proverbs 4:6

Proudly watching over New York Harbor and the nation, stands the majestic Statue of Liberty. Liberty is portrayed in this statue and elsewhere as a lady. Such a precious commodity as liberty is rightly given human attributes. It is fascinating that the book of Proverbs does a similar thing with wisdom. Wisdom too, is called a lady, and is portrayed with human characteristics.

In the above passage from Proverbs, Lady Wisdom promises to protect and watch over us. It is a promise given with a condition. We must first choose to love wisdom and not forsake her. Thus embraced, wisdom will bring protection and watch care over a people.

Biblically speaking, wisdom is looking at things from God's perspective and making the right choices based on that perspective. How critical it is for a nation that wants to experience God's protection to love and embrace wisdom! As the United States increasingly accepts a secular mindset and rejects divine revelation as a basis for our laws, we move farther away from the protection offered by wisdom.

Prayer Points

• Thank God for the gift of wisdom, and for the ability to see things from His perspective as we turn to His Word.

• Repent on behalf of our nation, because we have turned from making Scripture the basis of law, leaving behind wisdom, and looking to ourselves for truth.

• Cry out to the Lord, asking for godly wisdom to be loved and embraced once again by this nation.

My Prayer

I thank You, Lord, that You are a God of wisdom and revelation. You do not hide wisdom from us, but rather have told us that we only need to ask and You will freely give it. So, Father, we ask You for wisdom this day. We embrace the wisdom from above that allows us to see matters from Your perspective.

What we ask for ourselves personally, we also ask for our nation. Forgive us, Lord, for turning from Your ways and the wisdom that is Your Word. Our country has sought wisdom and direction from polls and surveys and other nations rather than looking to You. We have called Your wisdom "myth" and have called that which is foolishness "wisdom."

DAY FIVE

"But those who hope in the Lord will renew their strength. They will soar on wings like eagles; they will run and not grow weary, they will walk and not be faint." –Isaiah 40:31

The promise of renewed strength makes this a favorite Bible verse for many. The picture of a soaring eagle brings hope to those who are weary. For many years now, another soaring eagle has brought hope to many. The picture of America as a soaring eagle, proud, fast, moving above the clouds, has captured the imagination of millions, both in the United States and around the world.

But note that our verse today likens the eagle to those who hope in the Lord. Is that a picture of the United States today? It's a question not just for our government, but for us as citizens. Where is our hope? Is it in whomever currently occupies the White House or Congress? Is it in our military or economic strength?

There is nothing sadder than a crippled eagle, one that can no longer soar. Healing, however, can come to damaged wings. It involves the redirection of hope. The American eagle can soar again when we learn as a people to place our hope in the Lord.

Prayer Points

- Thank the Lord how the biblical picture of a soaring eagle fits the symbol of our nation.
- Ask the Lord to help you put your hope and trust in Him alone.
- Pray for our nation, that we would once again soar as an eagle as we place our trust in the Lord.

My Prayer

Father, I thank You for this picture from the prophet Isaiah of an eagle soaring and how well that helps me as I pray for my nation today. Forgive us, Lord, for the pride that has often marked us a nation. That pride has caused us to put our hope in our own strength and might and not in You. Forgive us. If we are to run and not grow weary as a nation, it will be only because we have turned back to You as our hope. Help us, Lord, to hope in You!

DAY SIX

"Surely God is my salvation; I will trust and not be afraid. The LORD, the LORD, is my strength and my song; he has become my salvation." –Isaiah 12:2

There are many things that can strike fear into the heart of a nation. In the years following the terrorist attacks of September 11, 2001, we have feared off-course planes, envelopes with white powder, and threats from extremists around the world. We take as many precautions as we can, all the while fearing that something, sometime will slip through and cause harm. Fear is tough to live with and causes a nation to react in manmade ways that are not always godly.

The Bible often warns us not to be afraid. The reason given is that God is our salvation. Salvation doesn't always refer to eternal life or heaven. It often means deliverance from the enemy. Psalm 32:7 says, "You are my hiding place; you will protect me from trouble and surround me with songs of deliverance." Isaiah reminds us that when a nation (or person) trusts in the Lord, He steps in and brings salvation. When we experience the Lord's deliverance, fear is replaced by songs of joy, as Isaiah declares in today's text. Has the Lord become your song?

Prayer Points

• Bring your fears to the Lord and lay them at His feet.
• Ask the Lord to help the United States to learn to trust Him for our salvation as a nation.
• Confess (agree with God) that the Lord is indeed the salvation for our nation.

My Prayer

Lord, I agree with Your Word that You are our salvation. I believe that for my nation. Help us as a nation to cast aside fear and trust in You. Lord, do a mighty work in the hearts of Your people in the United States that brings about a national shift in priorities and confidence. We trust in You, Lord. Become our strength and our song!

DAY SEVEN

"Do not be afraid of them; the LORD *your God himself will fight for you." —Deuteronomy 3:22*

Yesterday's devotion also addressed the vital topic of national fear. Fear can paralyze a nation, or cause it to react in inappropriate ways. President Franklin Roosevelt understood that. When addressing a nation mired in the Great Depression, he reminded the people that the only thing they had to fear was fear itself. God gives us a very direct command when faced with enemies: "Do not be afraid of them." Don't give in to fear!

There is a very real reason why Israel in Moses' day was commanded not to fear. God Himself had promised to step in and fight on their behalf. They still had many battles ahead of them, but God had agreed to intervene in those battles for them. This promise can only be appropriated when a nation has committed itself to honor God and follow His ways. Wouldn't it be great to live in a nation that had so aligned itself with the purposes of God that we could live without fear because God had determined to fight on our behalf?

Prayer Points

- Ask the Lord to pour out a spirit of repentance on our nation that we might become a nation committed to following His ways.
- Ask the Lord to help the United States to so line up with God's purposes that He will choose to fight on our behalf.
- Stand in prayer against all fear, whether in your own life or in the life of our nation.

My Prayer

Father, we turn from fear and turn to You. We indeed have enemies as a nation who seek our destruction. We have attempted to stand against them in our own strength, all the while rejecting Your lordship over us. Forgive us, Lord. Heal our land. Help us to turn back to You, so that You Yourself will fight for us.

DAY EIGHT

"You, O Lord, reign forever; your throne endures from generation to generation." –Lamentations 5:19

In December of 2000, I spent some time on top of the World Trade Center in New York City with some prayer warrior friends, praying over the city. I wouldn't have believed it then if you had told me that nine months later those towers would collapse. Something so big, solid, and sturdy should have lasted for many, many years. Yet we live in a world that, sometimes quickly and sometimes through the centuries, is disintegrating and passing away.

That's hard to hear when you speak of nations, especially if you happen to be praying for your own nation. Yet the testimony of history is that nations rise and nations fall. Certainly this gives urgency to our prayers for America. But it also causes us to realize that the reign of the Lord lasts far beyond any individual nation. In times of turmoil and change, we hold fast to the truth of God's Word: His rule is not dependent upon any nation. His throne endures forever.

Prayer Points

- Give thanks to the Lord for His everlasting rule over this world.
- Ask the Lord to awaken the church to the temporary nature of the nations and to the eternal nature of the reign of God.
- As you pray for the United States, ask the Lord to help us as a nation to fulfill His purposes for us.

My Prayer

Lord, what peace fills my heart as I consider Your eternal throne. In a world in which everything seems to change so fast, and so many things fade and fall, how good it is to know You never change. Your throne, Your rule, continues from generation to generation. There will never be a generation for which You are not Lord, even if that generation does not acknowledge You.

Even as we pray for our beloved nation, we realize that there will come a time when it ceases to exist. My prayer, Lord, is that before that time, we would fulfill the purposes You have for us. Help us, Lord, to be a nation that brings honor and glory to Your name!

DAY NINE

"'No weapon forged against you will prevail, and you will refute every tongue that accuses you. This is the heritage of the servants of the LORD, and this is their vindication from me,' declares the LORD." –Isaiah 54:17

We live in a day of terrible weaponry. A push of a button from far away can destroy whole cities. No longer is war confined to the combatants, but to entire populations. Years ago, President Ronald Reagan directed our military scientists to develop a shield to protect us, especially from nuclear attack. The "Star Wars" shield certainly could provide some protection, but couldn't keep us from all attacks.

What if there was something (Someone) who could shield us from all attack? The promise of God to His people is astonishing. No one would suggest this verse gives a nation some kind of divine protection from physical weaponry or attack. But men and women of God down through the years have stood upon this verse to handle the attacks of Satan and have experienced the astonishing protection of God. What if we began to pray prayers of spiritual protection over our nation? Could we as believers, in prayer, blunt the attempt of the Enemy to sideline our nation and remove us from our place in God's plan?

Prayer Points

- Thank the Lord for His promise of protection for the servants of the Lord.
- Ask the Lord to raise up a shield of protection over our nation.
- In the name of Jesus, resist the Enemy's attacks on the godly foundation of the United States.

My Prayer

Father, Your promises are always sure. Thank You that You give Your servants the privilege of walking in victory and refuting every word spoken against us. Now, Lord, help us in wisdom to do this on behalf of our nation. Lord, awaken Your people out of apathy and help us to stand against the attacks of Satan against our nation. Forgive us for our passivity. May no weapon of the Enemy prevail against our nation, but may every one of those weapons come to naught against our Shield and Deliverer!

DAY TEN

"For where your treasure is, there your heart will be also."
—Matthew 6:21

Years ago I heard a famous preacher tell about a conversation he had with the president of a South American nation. The president of that nation told the preacher that he had discovered the roots of the difference between the United States and his own nation: "Our ancestors came to these shores looking for gold, but your ancestors came looking for God." That's a profound difference. And probably a little distorted, in that certainly there were some early settlers in America who came looking for gold, too. But that leader was right in understanding that there was a solid segment of those who came to the American colonies with a sincere desire to seek God and religious freedom.

What are we seeking now as a nation? God or gold? All too often we have been known as a nation that is interested more in money and things than in God and people. This attitude has infected the church as well as the nation. There is no doubt that the love of money is one of the key idols in our nation, and is standing in the way of another great move of God in our midst. Where is your heart today? Your answer indicates where your treasure is.

Prayer Points

- Ask the Lord to reveal clearly to you where your treasure is.
- Pray for your heart to be clearly focused on the Lord.
- In Jesus' name, tear down the idol of mammon (money) that has taken up residence in America today.

Lord Jesus, You spoke so often about money and the danger it can represent to us. Yet, You also used the wealth of the rich to accomplish Your mission. Help us to walk in that biblical understanding of both the danger and blessing of money. Forgive us for making an idol out of money or material things. Especially, Lord, forgive us when such idolatry happens in Your church. Help us to live lives that are free from greed and coveting, that we might be a prophetic voice to our nation. May we become a nation that treasures You far more than we treasure gold.

DAY ELEVEN

"I have told you these things, so that in me you may have peace. In this world you will have trouble. But take heart! I have overcome the world." –John 16:33

Jesus often used words in ways that no one else would use them. For instance, in today's passage He puts together "peace" and "trouble." We would never put the two together. If we are having trouble, we think that our peace has gone. But Jesus has a much clearer perspective than our typical frantic thought processes.

Jesus knew that as long as we live in this world, there will always be trouble. It might be on an individual basis: our illnesses, relationships, finances, and so forth. Or it might be on a national platform: war, economic crisis, natural disasters, etc. It doesn't matter who you are or in what nation you live, you *will* have trouble.

The good news is that peace is possible in the midst of this trouble. This peace is not found in avoiding trouble, but in embracing the

Prince of Peace. The peace Jesus speaks of is found in Him and is literally a commodity given to those who follow Him. It is intended to mark His followers. His disciples will be those who have experienced His peace in their own lives and who seek to bring it to the nation in which they live.

Prayer Points

- Ask the Lord to fill you with His peace.
- Pray that you will be a person who brings the peace of Christ into the lives of others.
- Pray that the church in America will live in such a way that the peace of Christ comes into the councils of our nation.

My Prayer

Forgive me, Lord, when I walk in anxiety and stress, failing to allow Your peace to rule in my life. Breathe Your peace into my heart. Help me to bring that peace with me into every situation I face. Lord, may Your peace so pervade Your church in America that it begins to mark us as a nation. We understand that we live in a time of troubles. You told us it would be that way. Help us in a miraculous way to experience Your peace in the midst of trouble.

DAY TWELVE

"I wait for the LORD, my soul waits, and in his word I put my hope." —Psalm 130:5

I don't like to wait. There, I've said it. It's a major fault, not a minor one. I've gotten in more trouble from not waiting than from virtually anything else in my life. That's really sad when you consider how much in the Bible is written concerning the virtues and blessings that come from learning to wait upon the Lord.

I wonder if the same thing is true for a nation. We seem to be a country that doesn't like to wait. We rush about, going somewhere, even if it's wrong. We are a busy, impatient people, trampling over one another to get ahead and succeed, whatever success means to you or me.

What would it be like in a nation that has learned to wait upon the Lord? Perhaps we would pay less attention to the latest fad or news flash, and stay focused on the concern we heard about last week or last month. We would probably be a nation more interested in our history and in hearing stories from those who have lived some of that history. Stories of people who were making a real difference in life would take ascendance over the latest celebrity gossip or political scandal. We might even become a nation where contemplation isn't frowned upon as being old fashioned.

Ultimately, a nation that has learned to wait upon the Lord is a nation that has renewed its hope. No longer rushing about in response to the latest poll or whim, there is a dependence upon the Word of God and eternal matters. A sense of the solid and the stable replaces the fleeting fancies of our current status. Hope is removed from being a campaign slogan to being a lifestyle that centers on the Word of God.

Prayer Points

• Ask the Lord to help you learn to wait on Him.
• Pray for the church in America to begin to model the stable lifestyle of waiting on the Lord.
• Pray for a movement of the Spirit that creates a dramatic cultural

transformation in the United States, bringing about a nation that has learned to put its hope in the Word of God.

My Prayer

Lord, it isn't easy to wait. There are so many things to do. Forgive me for not waiting on You and running ahead to do those things that seemed good to me. Teach Your church to be a good model of those who do not rush into every trend or fashion but who have learned to wait upon You. Lord, show us how waiting on You is not inactivity but an active lifestyle of drawing near and of keeping our eyes upon You. May You so transform Your church that it flows over into the life of this nation. Slow us down, Lord. Teach us to wait on You, so that Your purposes and plans might be lived out in America.

DAY THIRTEEN

"When you go into battle in your own land against an enemy who is oppressing you, sound a blast on the trumpets. Then you will be remembered by the LORD your God and rescued from your enemies." –Numbers 10:9

The shock of September 11, 2001 was magnified by the fact that as a nation, we have not been attacked in our land for a very long time. At the time of the attack on Pearl Harbor, Hawaii was not yet a state. For an actual invasion we have to go back to the War of 1812. Of course, there was the Civil War, fought within our land, but by our own people. We are historically not used to living on a battlefield.

Today's Scripture speaks of fighting battles within our own land. Though written to Israel, there is certainly a spiritual principle for us today. And we need to hear it because we are indeed in a war in our own land. It is not melodramatic at all to declare that there is a war in the spirit realm for the soul of America. Years ago, someone once reportedly said, "America has the soul of a church." Is that how you would describe the soul of America today?

Scripture always portrays Satan as attempting to maneuver nations against the kingdom of God, and he is often successful. For many years, the godly foundation and prayers of the faithful kept our nation at least somewhat close to the purposes of God. This spiritual war, though, has intensified through the years, and we certainly find ourselves in a battle in our own land against an enemy who desires to oppress us.

The command of God is to sound a blast on the trumpets. Trumpet blasts typically called the Lord's people together for battle. But the blowing of trumpets (shofars) was also a call to prayer. In our day, I believe the two are merged into one. The trumpet is being blown to fight this battle on our knees. Our enemy is not flesh and blood, and we do not wage war with carnal weapons. This trumpet call is to intense prayer that glorifies Jesus, resists the Devil, and releases the power of God. Then we can have every expectation of the promise of God to be remembered and rescued.

Prayer Points

- Thank the Lord for His promise of remembering us and of rescuing us from our enemies.
- Ask the Lord to help strengthen the trumpet call to intensive prayer, so that it is heard throughout the church in the United States.
- Commit in prayer to stand against the attacks of the Enemy on our nation.

My Prayer

Father, forgive me for not always being aware of the war that is going on in our nation. Awaken me and all of Your people to the reality of what the Enemy is doing to destroy our foundations. Teach us to pray as You taught us to pray, so that we would be delivered from the Evil One. Help us, Lord, to heed the call of the trumpet to pray as never before. Show us the extent of the battles and help us not to wage war in the flesh but in the Spirit. Thank You, Lord, for Your promise to remember us and to rescue us!

DAY FOURTEEN

"Better a little with the fear of the LORD than great wealth with turmoil." –Proverbs 15:16

I s there a better picture of the truth of this passage than Charles Dickens' classic *A Christmas Carol*? You know the story. Poor Bob Cratchit with son Tiny Tim and the rest of their impoverished family are filled with joy and faith, contrasted with the miserable existence of wealthy Ebenezer Scrooge. The novel isn't so much against money as it is our attitude of holding on to it and failing to live a life that uses what we have for others. The Bible would call that failing to have a fear of the Lord.

The United States is in a curious place regarding wealth. We certainly have affluence that is virtually unimaginable. Many place a high value on obtaining money. Our ethics regarding the ways we obtain wealth are often highly suspect. Yet, for all our failings in this area, we are also a nation known for generosity.

We celebrate those who are able to give great financial gifts for charitable reasons. When tragedy strikes, the greatness of America's generosity kicks in. We have sent American dollars around the world to help those in need. We even provide tax credits for those who give charitably. Yet we can do better. Not just in giving, but in our attitudes toward wealth. More fear of God, less striving after wealth. That would be better!

Prayer Points

- Repent for any greed or wrong attitudes concerning money.
- Pray for an increased spirit of generosity in the church.
- Ask the Lord to pour out godly fear of the Lord throughout our land.

My Prayer

Father, I thank You for the way You have poured out abundance upon our nation. Forgive us for the ways we have often hoarded or squandered that wealth. Help us to see from heaven's perspective how wealth is to be viewed and used. Pour out the fear of the Lord that causes us to see all that we have as coming from You. Help us as a nation not to put our trust in our finances but in You. Give us an even greater spirit of generosity.

DAY FIFTEEN

"But God demonstrates his own love for us in this: While we were still sinners, Christ died for us." –Romans 5:8

Years ago there was a pop psychology book entitled *I'm Ok, You're Ok*. Along with many other such teachings, it has resulted in a nation in which everything is okay. Nobody should be judged unless they do something that really hurts someone else. And even then, he or she probably had a good reason for doing such a bad thing.

One of the casualties of such a belief is the concept of sin. Many churches have even quit talking about sin. It just sounds so judgmental! That practice is making it more and more difficult for Americans to accept the real gospel.

I say *real* gospel, because there is a gospel that is lacking in reality. It is a gospel that focuses solely on the love of God. But apart from an understanding of sin, that's no gospel at all. Telling people that God loves them fits American culture. We believe we are all worthy of love and we all ought to love each other, and isn't it good that God is in on this love thing too?

Romans 5:8 destroys this pop gospel. When we were at our worst and most unlovable, God's amazing love stepped in. Without an understanding of ourselves as sinners, completely unlovable, we will never understand or accept the cross. The good news (gospel) is that because we are sinners, God, in the most daring act of love the universe has ever seen, sent His Son to take the penalty for our sin. Love for God and for our nation will cause us to proclaim the real gospel to those who desperately need to hear.

Prayer Points

- Thank the Lord for demonstrating His great love for you by dying for you while you were still a sinner.
- Pray for the preachers of America to fearlessly proclaim the Word of God regarding sin and God's love.
- Pray for a movement of God's Spirit across America that opens hearts to receive the gospel.

Lord, I am in awe of Your amazing love that reached out to me while I was yet a sinner. Thank You for that good news! I ask that Christians around this nation would speak and live out the truth of the gospel daily. I pray for preachers who would stand fearlessly in their pulpits and proclaim the truth of Your Word concerning sin, righteousness, and judgment. Help us never to separate Your love from our desperate sinfulness.

10/15

DAY SIXTEEN

"Do not conform any longer to the pattern of this world, but be transformed by the renewing of your mind. Then you will be able to test and approve what God's will is—his good, pleasing and perfect will." –Romans 12:2

Our nation doesn't know it, but America needs the church. Not just as a bunch of good-deed doers, but as those who give direction for the future and preserve and protect in the present. We've not done this well, but that is the place in which God has put us. We are to be light, helping people (and nations) avoid the pitfalls of darkness. We are to be salt, both as seasoning and protection for our society.

The nation cannot afford a sidelined church, taken out by worldliness and confusion. The Apostle Paul commands believers to allow ourselves no longer to be conformed by worldly patterns, but rather to be transformed by the renewing of our minds. Only then we will understand the will of God, not just for our own lives, but so that we can be a prophetic voice to our nation. Sometimes the best way to pray for our nation is to pray for revival in the church!

Prayer Points

- Repent of the church's failure to be light and salt in our society.
- Pray for a transformation in the church through a renewing of our minds through the Word of God.
- Ask the Lord for the church to rise up with a strong prophetic voice for America.

My Prayer

Lord, forgive us, Your people, for our timidity, worldliness, and failure to be the light and salt that our nation desperately needs. Transform us! May Your Word bring lasting change to our minds and lifestyles. Help us then to speak with boldness as we understand more and more of Your will. Help us not so much to seek political power as to seek to speak Your wisdom into political situations.

10/16

DAY SEVENTEEN

"The wrath of God is being revealed from heaven against all the godlessness and wickedness of men who suppress the truth by their wickedness." –Romans 1:18

D o you suppose that the above verse, speaking of the wrath of God, is true for every nation except the United States? Is there some way that we are somehow exempt from the wrath of God? We don't like to think about this, but the truth of the matter is that there is no exempt nation. Godlessness and wickedness will attract the wrath of God, both for individuals as well as for a nation. When godlessness and wickedness are embraced by a nation, then the wrath of God will be directed against that nation.

In the last fifty years, we have seen a serious attempt at suppressing truth in the United States. An artificial wall of separation between church and state has been built with the intent of removing God completely from the public square. And this is just one of the ways that truth is suppressed. Because of this, according to the Word of God, the wrath of God is being revealed.

There are a number of ways we can pray over such situations. First, we ask that the wrath of God bring about its purpose of leading people to repentance. We should ask that our sufferings not be wasted, but be brought to their redemptive purposes. Second, we ask that God's truth be restored to public consciousness and acceptance. We begin to pray for a restoration of God's Word into public life in America, not in any sort of theocratic way, but so there be no divorce between the spiritual and the secular.

Prayer Points

- Repent on behalf of our nation because we have allowed the suppression of God's truth.
- Pray that God's wrath on the wicked will bring about repentance.
- Ask the Lord for a holy boldness in the church to stand for truth in our nation.

My Prayer

Father, I tremble as I read Your Word today. I fear for my nation as I see godlessness and wickedness on the rise and the increased suppression of truth. I pray for mercy in the midst of Your wrath. Pour out a spirit of repentance upon the ungodly. Turn their hearts to You. As Your church sees Your wrath poured out, I pray that we will be those who tremble at Your Word and draw near to You in intimacy. Give us boldness to stand for truth and not to shrink back.

DAY EIGHTEEN

*"Honor the L*ORD *with your wealth, with the firstfruits of all your crops" —Proverbs 3:9*

God never has and never will need our wealth. He owns the cattle on a thousand hills. He is spirit and needs none of the things we need. Giving to the Lord has never been about His needs, but ours. We need to honor the Lord with our wealth.

Giving to God starts in Genesis and continues through Revelation. It is built into how we relate to God. Giving back to God is about restoring our understanding of God as our provider. It places us firmly under His care and lordship.

When the church in a nation tithes to God and recognizes His provision, that nation is blessed. God is honored, and we find ourselves in a place where God can begin to trust us with more because we are correctly using what He has already given us. Have you ever considered that much of our nation's economic turbulence might be caused by the failure of the Lord's people to honor Him with their wealth? The average Christian gives 2.7 percent to his or her church! What might happen in our nation as we offer ourselves and our wealth back to the Lord?

- Ask the Lord if you are properly honoring Him with your wealth.
- Pray for a spirit of generosity to well up within the church in America.
- Pray for God to be honored in this nation as we give abundantly and with right attitudes to Him.

My Prayer

Father, I thank You that You are the giver of every good and perfect gift. All that we have comes from Your hand. I am grateful to You. Help me, Lord, to honor You with my wealth, and to give back with a joyful spirit. Please pour out a spirit of generosity within the lives of Your people, so that You might be honored and our nation might be blessed.

DAY NINETEEN

"You will seek me and find me when you seek me with all your heart." –Jeremiah 29:13

Can you even imagine living in a nation where we talk about seeking the Lord together as a people? It certainly has happened before in the United States. From presidents to preachers, we have employed this sort of language through the years to describe the spiritual longing we should have for our Creator. But somewhere along the line we quit seeking. Even those who should have known better did not pusue God with their whole heart.

Today, not just the nation, but even the church has ceased to seek the Lord. I know that sounds like a harsh statement, but if we were seeking, we would be finding. That's the promise of God. It is time for repentance on the part of the people of God. We have failed to go after the Lord with our whole hearts. We have held on to doctrines and tradition but failed to pursue the Lord Himself. Like the church at Ephesus referred to in Revelation, we work hard and believe right things but have lost our first love.

God is not hiding. He desires to be found. But His people are so caught up in so many others things that we have forgotten our first love. We must repent and turn. It is time for another Great Awakening in our nation that begins with those who commit to seek the Lord with all their hearts.

Prayer Points

- If you are not seeking the Lord with your whole heart, this is the time to cry out in repentance.
- Pray for a spirit of repentance to fall upon the church in America that would cause us to turn back to God and seek Him.
- Pray for bold leaders who begin to speak in all spheres of life of the need to seek the Lord.

My Prayer

Lord, forgive me for getting caught up in so many activities and things that I have failed to put You first. Give me a seeking heart. Help me not to be content with anything less than You Yourself. What I ask for myself, I ask for the whole church. May our church services be filled with the weeping of those who realize how we have failed to seek You passionately. Help us to be a people desperate for Your presence and not content with anything else. Please raise up those in every aspect of life who will call for and model the seeking life.

DAY TWENTY

10/19

"Be strong and courageous. Do not be afraid or terrified because of them, for the LORD your God goes with you; he will never leave you nor forsake you." –Deuteronomy 31:6

One of the marks of the end of the age is fear. Scriptures warn us that the hearts of men will fail them with all the pressures and terrors they will face. We certainly live in an age of fear and anxiety. Millions of Americans are helped through their fears through therapy, while others are made better through medication. Whether it is an internal anxiety or brought on by the struggles of our nation, fear seems to be on the rise.

In marked contrast are the followers of the Prince of Peace, whose lives are ruled by His peace. To be sure, many Christians have failed to grab hold of the promises of peace, but that failure does not discount the power of the promise. Over and over in the Word we are told not to be afraid because the Lord is with us. The Lord's presence allows us to face our fears with courage.

We will need courage to face the battles ahead of us in our nation. For too long the church has been timid and passive, afraid to stand against the attacks of the Enemy. Our nation cannot afford a silent church, afraid to speak truth into the issues of the day. The Lord speaks loudly to us today, "Be strong and courageous!"

Prayer Points

• Confess any fears you may have to the Lord. Turn them over to Him.

• Thank the Lord for His promise never to leave us or forsake us.

• Pray for a spirit of courage to rise within the church.

My Prayer

Father, forgive me for my fears. I hear You say in Your Word again and again, "Do not be afraid." Today, I cast all my anxiety on You because You care for me. I hold onto the promises of Your peace. With Your presence, Lord, I choose courage as a way of life. Please pour that spirit of courage into the life of Your church in America. Help us to rise up in truth against the evils of our age. Help us to live in such a way that we are able courageously to model Your life, Lord Jesus, in the midst of our world.

DAY
TWENTY-ONE

"Let us fix our eyes on Jesus, the author and perfecter of our faith, who for the joy set before him endured the cross, scorning its shame, and sat down at the right hand of the throne of God." —Hebrews 12:2

We often forget that it was the politics of His day that were the immediate cause of Jesus' death. The Roman occupation of Israel, coupled with the jockeying for power among several Jewish sects, created a tension that simply couldn't allow for a popular miracle-working preacher who offended all of the powers that were present. Much of Jesus' teaching dealt with how to live in such a politically tense situation.

So in our day, as we struggle sometimes with even knowing how to pray for our nation, this is a critical command to embrace: Fix your eyes on Jesus. We don't have to do this on our own. Jesus understands political and national situations and struggles. As we pray for our nation, we keep our eyes fixed on Him.

As we look at the rest of Hebrews 12:2, we are reminded how hard it was for Jesus as He struggled with the political system of His day. It led to a cross. We aren't assuming that because we are praying for our nation that everything will immediately get better and we will all live happily ever after. Our prayers can make a difference! But we may pay a price. Jesus endured the cross because He saw beyond it to the fulfillment of the Father's purposes. We fix our eyes on Jesus, praying for our nation, committed to enduring whatever may come, in order to see the fulfillment of the Lord's purposes in our day.

Prayer Points

- Thank the Lord for enduring the cross on our behalf.
- In prayer, fix your eyes on Jesus. Ask Him to show you how to pray for our nation.
- Commit to enduring whatever it takes to see the fulfillment of God's purposes in our nation.

My Prayer

Lord, today and always I choose to fix my eyes upon You. You lived in a land of political tensions and struggles and overcame, though at a great cost. Teach me how to pray and how to live in the midst of the battles we are facing as a nation. Give me the courage that You had to endure whatever comes in order to please the Father and see His purposes fulfilled.

10/21

DAY
TWENTY-TWO

"Do not let your hearts be troubled. Trust in God;
trust also in me." —John 14:1

What is troubling your heart today? When the disciples first heard those words, they were worried because Jesus told them He was leaving. That really caused them great anxiety. But Jesus wanted them to trust Him.

So, is there something about our nation that has you worried today? The economy, racial tension, decisions (or indecisions) in Washington, D.C., the terrorist threats? The list could get long. How can we not have troubled hearts?

Jesus gets really practical here with His Word to us: Don't have a troubled heart; instead, trust Me. He doesn't just tell us not to be worried, which doesn't work unless there is something that can replace the worry. And that's right where Jesus places Himself. "Trust Me," He says. Such trust will be lived out in us as we pray. Are you anxious and troubled about our nation? Take your concerns to Jesus. Trust Him. Worrying isn't trust; it's foolishness. Intercession is trust in action. So, take the issues of this nation that are troubling you and you bring them to Jesus. Let Him deal with them. He can! Do you believe that?

Prayer Points

• Jesus doesn't want us to have a troubled heart. Confess what is troubling your heart today.

- Ask Him to help you trust Him.
- Now, in trust, bring the issues of our nation that trouble you and lay them at His feet.

My Prayer

Lord, it is very easy to have a troubled heart as I look at my nation. We are so divided, and it looks like nothing can bridge the growing divide. It seems like daily there are news stories which indicate that we are moving farther and farther away from the standards of Your Word and Your righteousness. No one seems to have the answers we need.

So, Lord Jesus, I turn to You. I trust You. What no political party or individual can do, I believe You can do. Would You step into this situation and bring about Your righteous purposes? I trust You. I choose not to have a troubled heart, but will instead entrust my nation to You.

DAY
TWENTY-THREE

"Have nothing to do with the fruitless deeds of darkness, but rather expose them." –Ephesians 5:11

It seems that most of the serious political scandals have involved cover ups. It wasn't always the misdeed that was the worst, so much as the lying and manipulation of trying to hide it from the public. Cover ups always try to keep things in darkness, away from the light where people can really see what has happened.

Followers of Jesus ought to really hate cover ups. We are called to be children of the light, avoiding the deeds of darkness. I think we have often misunderstood what it means to be light. Light by its nature shines. Darkness simply flees. It disappears when light appears. If our nation is in darkness, why? What has happened to the light? Darkness doesn't push back light. It is simply the absence of light. It's time to shine, church. It's time for the light of Christ to be lived out in our neighborhoods, schools, and cities. We don't need to rail against the darkness; we just need to shine. The Light of the world lives within us, and our nation desperately needs His light to shine in every dark corner.

Prayer Points

• Ask the Lord to forgive you for hiding your light.
• Ask the Lord to shine so brightly through you today that others will see Him in all that you do.
• Pray for an explosion of light in the church, bringing transformation to our communities.

My Prayer

Thank You, Light of the World, for coming to live in me. Shine brightly in me today. Forgive me for hiding Your light. Forgive me for the times when I preferred the shadows to the brilliance of Your presence. Shine through Your church in America. Help us to live and to love as You did, so that the darkness in our land will flee and Your light will shine.

DAY
TWENTY-FOUR

"Who among you fears the LORD and obeys the word of his servant? Let him who walks in the dark, who has no light, trust in the name of the LORD and rely on his God."
—Isaiah 50:10

The Bible tells us that the fear of the Lord is the beginning place for wisdom. That just might qualify us for being one of the least wise places ever. We don't talk much about the fear of the Lord, even in our churches. Worse than that, we don't live in the fear of the Lord.

Isaiah helps us understand what it means to be someone who fears the Lord. It is the person who obeys what God says. Such a person understands that God knows what is best and will endeavor to do what the Lord commands. He or she fears what happens when the Word of the Lord is ignored.

We live in a day when even something as basic as the Ten Commandments is being removed from public places. This is simply foolish. Perhaps it is time once again to begin to teach and preach about the fear of the Lord.

Prayer Points

- Come before the Lord, confessing that you are one who fears Him.
- Ask Him for the strength of His Holy Spirit to enable you to obey His Word.

• Pray for a fresh wave of the fear of the Lord to fall upon the church in America.

My Prayer

Father, I come before You with fear and trembling. It is because of Your great mercy and love that I fear You. I know You are always right in Your judgments. Help me to be one who obeys Your Word. Enable me through Your Spirit to do what I hear. Help me not to be just a hearer of the Word, but a doer. Lord, our nation needs the moral and spiritual backbone of a people who fear You and obey Your Word. May the fear of the Lord fall upon Your people in our day!

DAY
TWENTY-FIVE

"Learn to do right! Seek justice, encourage the oppressed. Defend the cause of the fatherless, plead the case of the widow." –Isaiah 1:17

I love the church, so, it isn't easy for me to say this: Church, our reputation stinks! We are thought of as hypocrites, haters, critics, and irrelevant. Unfortunately, all those descriptive words are accurate. Of course, there are other words I could use to describe what I have seen in the church: love, sacrifice, giving, and compassion, for example.

You see, the church is so large that there are millions of us in different stages of growth and maturity. So, it's not surprising, really, to see such a vast difference in the ways we act and are perceived. Yet, God has given us an important mandate that few of us are fulfilling. We are the body of Christ on earth. How can we overcome our poor reputation?

Here's a simple suggestion: Learn to do right! Especially when it comes to those who are hurting and helpless. The church must emulate Jesus who always sought out the least and the lowest. If we listen to Isaiah and seek justice, encourage the oppressed, defend the cause of the fatherless and plead the case of the widow, we would be thought of in a much better way in our society. We might not have such nice buildings or such fancy programs, but our reputation would surely be better. And our nation would be changed!

Prayer Points

- Repent over the poor reputation of the church in our nation.
- Ask the Lord to show you those who are hurting and need you to reach out to them with the love of Jesus.
- Pray for a spirit of compassion to come over the church in the United States so that we will begin seriously to live out the lifestyle of Jesus in our communities.

My Prayer

Lord, forgive us. We have so often made church about us and our needs and wants. In the process we have ignored those who were hurting right down the street from our buildings. Please help us to see people, really see them, as You do. Help us to learn to do right as Isaiah told us. Remake us in Your image, Lord Jesus. You went to those who desperately needed You. May Your compassion well up within us to meet the needs of those around us.

DAY
TWENTY-SIX

"Joshua told the people, 'Consecrate yourselves, for tomorrow the LORD will do amazing things among you.'" –Joshua 3:5

Who of us would not like to see the Lord do amazing things in our midst? We certainly need that supernatural work of God in our nation today. Israel received that promise; yet, it was a conditional promise. God would do miraculous things if His people consecrated themselves.

Consecration is one of those "church words" that sometimes confuses us. To *consecrate* is to set apart for a particular purpose. It is closely tied to the idea of being made holy. In the tabernacle and later the temple, certain items were consecrated for a special purpose. They could no longer be used in an ordinary way. That was God's Word to the Israelites in Joshua's day. It is also God's Word to us today.

Our nation desperately needs a consecrated church, a people set aside for the Lord's purposes. We are the way God has chosen to communicate His will to nations. But if we are not a consecrated, holy people, the communication becomes garbled and mixed with our unholiness.

Note that the Lord said that they (and we) were to consecrate themselves. This was not a passive thing, but actively required them to set themselves apart for the purposes of God. As you pray today, would you consecrate yourself, so that we might see the Lord do amazing things in our midst?

Prayer Points

- Repent of a lack of consecration and purpose in your life.
- Commit yourself to a life of consecration for the Lord's purposes.
- Pray for a spirit of consecration and holiness to come upon the church in America.

My Prayer

Father, I am so grieved over my lack of consecration. I have believed and loved You, but I've been trying to do Your work in my own strength, and so often for my own purposes. In the name of Jesus, I consecrate myself unto Your purposes. Here I am, Lord. Use me as You will. And what I pray for myself, I pray for Your church. Lord, help us to be holy. Our nation desperately needs a holy people to speak Your Word in these days. Pour out Your Holy Spirit upon us that we might be empowered to be used by You. Lord, we need You to do amazing things in our midst.

DAY TWENTY-SEVEN

*"It is for freedom that Christ has set us free.
Stand firm, then, and do not let yourselves be burdened
again by a yoke of slavery." –Galatians 5:1*

Freedom has a high value in the kingdom of God—not a freedom to do as you please, but, rather, a freedom to please God. That's important for us to understand as we pray for our nation.

In handling Scripture accurately, we must point out that the freedom Paul spoke of to the Galatians was freedom from laws and traditions that kept people bound spiritually. This principle of freedom has been used across the centuries to set people free from other kinds of bondage and slavery. Freedom is a gift of God and is to be treasured.

As you pray for the United States, pray that the spirit of freedom would be rekindled. Paul encouraged the Galatians to "stand firm" against any attempt to take away their freedom. There are certainly many today who fear that our freedom to live lives pleasing to God is being eroded by growing governmental control over many aspects of our lives. Praying for freedom is praying a kingdom value into our nation.

Prayer Points

• Pray for vigilance over any erosion of freedom.
• Thank the Lord for the freedom we have in Christ.
• Pray that we will not again be burdened with the yoke of slavery.

My Prayer

I thank You, Lord, that You have set us free from bondage. I'm so grateful for the freedom we have in Christ. I thank You for the Founders of our nation who built that love and respect for freedom into the core of who we are. Help us, Lord, to be vigilant against the erosion of freedom. Build a love of freedom into our churches and schools and other formative institutions. Give us the courage and boldness to stand firm against those who would take away freedom. May we always be the land of the free.

DAY
TWENTY-EIGHT

10/27

"Then you will know the truth, and the truth will set you free." –John 8:32

There is nothing more powerful than a well-told lie. Individuals can find their lives spinning out of control because they believe something untrue about themselves or someone close to them. We're all aware of how that can happen to a nation when we look back at the propaganda ministry of Nazi Germany and the deception that filled a country. It doesn't surprise us that Jesus called Satan a liar.

The one thing that is more powerful than the lie, though, is the truth, clearly and forcefully stated. It is truth that sets us free and keeps us free. That is true spiritually, and is certainly true for a nation. When we receive the truth, both about our own sinfulness as well as God's great love for us expressed through Jesus Christ, we are set free. We must continue to hold to this great truth all of our lives.

A nation must believe truth as well. The authors of our Declaration of Independence appealed to certain self-evident truths. A love of truth is seen as essential to our rights and liberty. In these days, it seems that truth often takes a backseat to partisan bickering and positioning. Those who pray for the nation must learn to love truth and pray for it to come forth in power.

- Pray for truth to become valued again in American society.
- Pray specifically for truth to be an established standard in our news media.
- Pray for a love for God's truth to grow in the church.

My Prayer

I thank You, Lord Jesus, that You are the Truth! And it is You, the Truth, that sets men free. Thank You for the freedom we have in You. I thank You that so many of our founding fathers in this nation understood that freedom ultimately is a gift from You and therefore is dependent upon Your truth. Please restore truth to our nation. Help us to quit believing lies. Lord, expose lies! Bring a fresh love for truth to those who report the news. Give discernment to those who watch, listen, or read the news, so that truth might always prevail.

DAY
TWENTY-NINE

"'Nevertheless, I will bring health and healing to it; I will heal my people and will let them enjoy abundant peace and security." –Jeremiah 33:6

There is a real wave of discouragement and despondency sweeping through the United States these days. For many, it seems as though our nation is on the path of no return. There is a real concern that we have drifted too far from God and that we might never again see a nationwide spiritual awakening. It certainly is possible for a people to go too far in their rebellion.

But I do not believe the United States is yet at that point. The Lord has many who are crying out to Him. There is a growing movement of prayer that is focusing on repentance and turning back to God. Check out this website: *OneCry.com* for an encouraging viewpoint.

God's Word to Judah many years ago was both bad news and good news. The people were going to suffer for their rebellion against God. But in the midst of those tough times, God made a promise showing that He wasn't done with Judah. He promised health, peace, and security to a people who didn't deserve it. But such is His mercy and love—both then and today!

Prayer Points

• Make a commitment to pray daily for a spirit of repentance to come upon the church in the United States.
• Thank the Lord that His mercy triumphs over judgment.
• Pray for healing, peace, and security to come to this nation.

My Prayer

Lord, we certainly deserve Your judgment. As a nation, we have sinned against You in virtually every way. We have deliberately tried to remove You from public life. We have squandered wealth, chosen convenience over life, abused the weak, dishonored the poor, and allowed our prejudices and hatreds to divide us. Forgive us! Instead of judgment, pour out Your mercy. We need the healing that only You can provide. Bring again to our nation Your health, Your peace, and Your security.

DAY THIRTY

"You, my brothers, were called to be free. But do not use your freedom to indulge the sinful nature; rather, serve one another in love." —Galatians 5:13

When Christ set men free from the law, not everyone knew what to do with their freedom. Some literally taught that freedom in Christ meant everything was permissible, even those things that were morally wrong. Paul, who understood freedom perhaps better than anyone, had to step in and provide some corrective teaching.

Freedom is a great thing. Knowing how to use our freedom is even better. History is replete with examples of those who failed to understand the purposes and restraints of freedom. The violence and despotism associated with the French Revolution is a good example of freedom gone bad. Their rejection of the Christian faith prevented the tempering effect that faith should have had on passions that were given new-found freedom.

Over the past few decades there has been a growing movement in the United States desiring to remove any restraints that faith might provide. There is a world of difference between freedom of religion and freedom from religion. Though the latter uses the word "freedom," it nonetheless is a path that leads away from freedom and toward tyranny and intolerance.

Prayer Points

• Thank the Lord for the freedom we have in Him and for the wisdom to understand that freedom.

- Ask the Lord to thwart the efforts of those who would remove religious freedom from our nation.
- Pray for a new spirit of responsible freedom to sweep through our nation.

My Prayer

I thank You, Lord, for the freedom we have in Jesus. Help us to use that freedom with the wisdom that comes from above. Protect freedom in our nation. Lord, step in and prevent those who oppose You from gaining power or influence in this nation. Help our schools and universities to teach and model what it means to be responsible with the freedom that has been given us.

DAY
THIRTY-ONE

"For where you have envy and selfish ambition, there you find disorder and every evil practice." –James 3:16

The Bible is so very practical. Since God created and knows us so well, when we read His Word it's a bit like reading the owner's manual for humans. His commands and instructions are built on a complete understanding of what works and doesn't work, both within us and in our relationships with others.

James speaks with authority and insight as he points out what will happen to a society or group when people begin to envy each other and to have ambition that puts self ahead of others. The result is a breakdown of society in which you find disorder and all kinds of evil practices. This can and does happen in local churches, social groups, and so forth. As bad as that is, it becomes even more devastating when it happens at a national level.

I watched the news right before writing this devotional. James pegged it! I saw disorder and every evil practice at a national level, and it all goes back to envy and selfish ambition. Ultimately, this is a spiritual problem and the only solution is spiritual. America needs Jesus and needs Him badly!

Prayer Points

- Ask the Lord to reveal if you are holding on to any envy or selfish ambition. If so, repent of it now.
- Pray for the salvation of those who are in leadership of our nation. Ask the Lord to remove all envy and selfish ambition.
- Pray that the church in America will be set free from all envy and selfish ambition.

My Prayer

Thank You, Lord, for Your Word that so clearly shows us for who we are and Who You are. Keep me, Lord, from envy and selfish ambition. May Your church be a model to this nation of what it means to live without these horrible sins. I pray today for our national leaders, that every one of them would come to know You, Lord Jesus, as Savior and Lord of their lives. Lord, remove from them the envy and selfish ambition that so easily attaches itself to those in places of political power. Father, we stand against the disorder and evil practices that are increasingly characterizing our land. Bring Your godly peace and righteousness to America!

10/31

DAY
THIRTY-TWO

"But seek first his kingdom and his righteousness, and all these things will be given to you as well." —Matthew 6:33

Many have referred to the Sermon on the Mount as Jesus' manifesto for kingdom living. It certainly is a call to a radical lifestyle such as the world has never seen. It covers most of the major areas of life and brings everything under the lordship of Jesus. One of the best known and most powerful statements is our text today: "Seek first his kingdom and his righteousness, and all these things will be given to you as well."

In a culture that is continually striving for more and more, these are radical words. Rather than focusing on our clothes, our food, or our shelter, Jesus said our focus must be on the things of God. My wife, Kim, delights in telling the story of the Christmas morning when our son, David, just a toddler at the time, was playing with his first present. When he received a second present, he politely said, "No thank you. I already have one." Is it possible for us to have that sort of innocence that trusts in the Lord, not grasping for more, but contented with what we have?

With a proper focus on the kingdom of God, we will live in a nation that can care for those who are hurting and still have an abundance. This will happen not because the government has mandated (that has never worked) but because we are seeking first that which is eternal and are then content to allow the Lord to provide everything else that we need.

Prayer Points

- Commit yourself in prayer to seeking first His kingdom and His righteousness.
- Pray for that spirit of seeking God to pervade the church in America.
- Pray for a right focus in America—back to the Lord and away from material things.

My Prayer

Lord Jesus, I commit myself this day to seeking Your kingdom and Your righteousness. With all that is in me, I long to experience Your rule over my life. May that same desire permeate the church in America. Give us seeking hearts that will not be content with anything less than You and Your kingdom in our lives. With that firmly in place, help us to trust You to provide for us in every way. Help our nation to be set free from a grasping materialism that is never satisfied and never secure. May our national motto "In God we trust" become a way of life for America.

DAY
THIRTY-THREE

"The people living in darkness have seen a great light; on those living in the land of the shadow of death a light has dawned." –Matthew 4:16

The Apostle Matthew reached back into the Old Testament to comment on the coming of Messiah to His people, lost in darkness and death. It is a beautiful picture of light coming to shine in the darkest of places. The arrival of Jesus brought life and light and forever changed the world wherever that light has shone.

The light of Jesus not only comes to bring transformation to those who have never heard, but also to those in whom the light has grown dim. In so many ways, the United States has been blessed by the gospel of Jesus Christ. From east to west, from north to south, the good news of Jesus has been proclaimed and churches have been established. Yet, generations have come and gone, and in many places the light of Christ has almost gone out. Some churches no longer preach the Bible. In other places, a different culture has arisen in neighborhoods where there is no longer a church effectively reaching out to its community.

We need to see that our America needs the light of Christ once again. It is time to proclaim to those dwelling in darkness that the Light has come! To see true transformation in the nation will require massive church planting and church revitalization. Those dwelling (in America) in the land of the shadow of death must hear the good news that a light has dawned in our land once again.

Prayer Points

- Pray that churches in your community and area will preach the gospel of Christ powerfully.
- Pray for church planting movements in our nation.
- Ask the Lord to bring revival to the church in America.

My Prayer

Father, our nation desperately needs the light of the gospel once again. In so many places, a stagnant church has made the good news seem like stale old news. Forgive us for not handling correctly what has been entrusted to us. Bring new life and light to Your church. Revive Your people once again, Lord. I pray that from that new life, Your light would shine into places of darkness in this nation. I pray for a massive church planting movement within this nation and another Great Awakening of souls coming to You.

DAY THIRTY-FOUR

"But the needy will not always be forgotten, nor the hope of the afflicted ever perish." –Psalm 9:18

The earliest Christians were basically poor. There were a few wealthy individuals, but the good news of Jesus was especially attractive to the down and out. Jesus went out of His way to minister to the poor and needy. Those who were ill received special attention. The earliest disciples of Jesus followed His example by reaching out to the hurting.

An interesting thing happened. Within generations, those who followed Jesus prospered. There is something about the life of Christ that encourages hard work, thriftiness, generosity, and the sort of characteristics that bring about a greater prosperity. Oh, I don't mean every Christian ends up wealthy. That's just not true. But there is definitely a trend of what we might call upward mobility over the generations for many Christian families in America.

The danger we often face is forgetting from whence we came. It is easy for us to forget that generations ago our families might have been those struggling just to make it. So God's Word is filled with reminders that God is always watching out for the needy and the afflicted. He wants us to do so as well, for He has blessed us to be a blessing to others in physical, material and spiritual ways. If we would faithfully follow Jesus in this way, there would be no need for the government to take care of those in need. God wants His people to get serious about being His hands, feet and voice in our families, our communities and in our nation!

Prayer Points

• Begin to pray for those you know who are hurting financially and physically, and ask God to show you how to respond.
• Pray for a humility and an outreach in the church toward those whom the Bible calls the least among us.
• Repent of any negative attitudes you may have had toward the poor or afflicted.

My Prayer

Father, I am so thankful that You do not show favoritism. Help me to be like You. Give me a compassion from You for those who are poor or afflicted in any way. Show me not only how to pray but how You might want me to follow my prayers with actions. Lord, please pour out that attitude upon all Your people. May Your church rise up in compassion and good deeds to minister to those who are hurting in every way in our nation. Forgive us, Lord, for allowing or expecting the government to do this work that really belongs to us.

DAY
THIRTY-FIVE

"For we must all appear before the judgment seat of Christ, that each one may receive what is due him for the things done while in the body, whether good or bad." –2 Corinthians 5:10

I remember the day, more than thirty years ago, when I had to stand before a judge to hear his judgment. At issue was an argument over whether or not I lived in the right district to run for a particular elective office. Even though I had not done anything wrong, I still felt very anxious. No one likes to hear judgment passed on them. (By the way, I won that case.)

We don't like to think about judgment. But Scripture is very clear that every person on the planet will stand before Christ to be judged. Though our salvation is dependent upon whether or not Christ is our Savior and Lord, our actions as individuals in life certainly factor into things eternally in a way that we don't fully comprehend.

How does knowing this fact change the way you pray for governmental leaders and those in authority when you recognize that they, too, must stand before the judgment seat of Christ? We are not called to be accusers, but intercessors. The picture of the judgment seat of Christ should drive us to our knees in passionate prayer for our leaders and many others.

Prayer Points

• Thank the Lord for paying the price for your redemption and that your judge is also your Savior!

- Pray for the salvation of local government leaders.
- Pray for the salvation of national government leaders.

My Prayer

Father, I know that You are the Ultimate Judge over all mankind and that You have turned judgment over to Your Son, Jesus, our Lord and Savior. Thank You. Lord, I face judgment without fear because of Your love for me that brought me into Your family and forgave all of my sins. But, Lord, I fear for the many who do not know You and face a fearful judgment. Help me to pray for those who so desperately need You. I pray especially for those who are in authority over us at a national level. Their actions are so visible to a watching world and so often are contrary to Your revealed Word. Bring conviction of sin and draw them near to You that they might face judgment with the peace of Christ in their hearts.

DAY
THIRTY-SIX

"Keep them and do them, for that will be your wisdom and your understanding in the sight of the peoples, who, when they hear all these statutes, will say, 'Surely this great nation is a wise and understanding people.' For what great nation is there that has a god so near to it as the LORD our God is to us, whenever we call upon him? And what great nation is there, that has statutes and rules so righteous as all this law that I set before you today?" –Deuteronomy 4:6–8, ESV

What makes a nation great? Its military forces or its growing economy? Is it great natural resources or an industrious people? All of those and more certainly contribute to the greatness that nations strive for. But the Bible shows us a different perspective. It's a fascinating national concept found buried deep in this Old Testament passage. The greatness of a nation is directly related to the righteousness of its laws and rules.

As our nation began, our laws were made in recognition of God. Even though a number of our founding fathers were not church-going Christians, they all had a respect for the laws of God and literally based the new nation's laws upon what they considered divine law. God blessed their decision, and greatness was achieved.

Over the years the making and understanding of law has drifted from that strong godly perspective. Increasingly, lawmakers are looking to other nations or cultural trends for guidelines in laws. It could be argued that our greatness as a nation is drifting with that trend. It is time to begin praying for a return to laws that have their basis in God's Word.

Prayer Points

• Thank God for a good foundation for this nation in the nature of its laws.
• Pray for a return to that solid foundation.
• Pray for the judges of this nation, that they would seek the wisdom that comes from above.

My Prayer

Father, when I read the founding documents of our nation, I give thanks to You for the wisdom given to the men who wrote them. They clearly tried to base their writings on Your revelation. Would You pour out that wisdom on those who are currently in leadership in our nation? We have been drifting from Your Word, and our laws are increasingly in opposition to Your revealed will. Turn us, Lord. Line our laws up with Your Word so that we might once again achieve greatness as a nation because we reflect what You desire.

DAY
THIRTY-SEVEN

"I pray that you may be active in sharing your faith, so that you will have a full understanding of every good thing we have in Christ." —Philemon 1:6

It's easy to criticize our government. There's a lot going wrong in Washington, D.C. If a representative government has gone wrong, however, that means our problems are deeper than just our leaders. It's a reflection of our condition as a nation. Spiritually speaking then, it goes back to a problem with the church in our nation.

In a very real sense, the church in America has become lax and unfocused in our work. We have made the church about us and our desires, when we were always intended to be about reaching out and making a difference in our culture. Hiding behind church walls is a good way to bring about not only a slow death for the church but also a steady decline in a nation.

Paul's admonition to Philemon is not only good for church growth but for the renewal of a nation. *All* Christians must be active in sharing their faith. If tens of millions of us in the United States take these words to heart, we will see a turn around in the spiritual condition of our nation. Quit complaining! Begin to pray and share your faith and see what God does.

Prayer Points

- Ask the Lord to forgive you for your failure to actively share your faith.
- Ask the Lord to show you the next steps you need to take in sharing your faith.
- Pray for a fresh wave of evangelism to sweep over America.

My Prayer

Father, forgive me for my timidity when it comes to sharing my faith. Give me the boldness I need, along with wisdom to actively share my faith as a way of life. Lord, I pray that there will indeed be a fresh wave of evangelism that will flow from Your people out over this nation. Bring millions into Your kingdom! Change the hearts of many in this nation. You are our hope, Lord! Forgive us for looking to the government to change things, when all along You were ready and willing to change hearts. Change us, Lord, from the inside out.

11/06

DAY
THIRTY-EIGHT

"What good is it for a man to gain the whole world, yet forfeit his soul?" –Mark 8:36

The heroes of America are often those who began with nothing, but through hard work, made a success of themselves. That success is normally gauged in terms of money, fame, or power. It is certainly true that hard work and success often (though not always) go together. What needs to be examined is the criteria by which we judge success.

Jesus warns us that the typical standard for success is insufficient. While not discounting the value of wealth, Jesus asks His typical style of question in which the answer is obvious. "What good is it for a man to gain the whole world, yet forfeit his soul?" No good at all! This simple question challenges our very basis for success.

What we need is a new image of an American hero. The individual who works hard to achieve success and experiences that success through a life of selfless service, compassionate care for others, and uncompromising worship of the Lord should be our hero. As we hold those individuals in high esteem, they become models to impact future generations to live for true eternal success.

Prayer Points

- Ask the Lord to show you clearly how you have measured success in yourself and others.
- Pray for a clarity of purpose in your life, with your focus on Jesus.
- Pray for the emergence of a new generation of American heroes who exemplify the kind of God-focused life that inspires others toward that same type of life.

My Prayer

Lord Jesus, I thank You for the way You speak so practically into our lives. You know how easy it is for us to get caught up in gaining material things. It is such a besetting sin here in America that we have made financial success a virtue. Forgive us for our misguided view of what success really is. Instead, Lord, help us to focus on living a life in You, for You, and then poured out on behalf of others. How dramatically our nation would be changed if we began to think of success in spiritual terms and not just in the accumulation of wealth, power or fame.

DAY
THIRTY-NINE

"This is the one I esteem: he who is humble and contrite in spirit, and trembles at my word." –Isaiah 66:2

All too often, Americans are looked at as arrogant or prideful. Years ago, there was a book entitled *The Ugly American* that told of how Americans in the Foreign Service often perpetuated that view. It is time for a new reputation for Americans; one that is in line with what God desires for all people.

The prophet Isaiah gives us an amazing perspective of what God is looking for in us. The individual that God esteems is humble, contrite in spirit, and trembles at His Word. Before we just nod in passive agreement and move on, consider for a moment if that is the way we are wanting our children to grow up. So often, even as Christians, we want our children to be outgoing and confident, so much so that we wink at a little bit of pride. Pride is a deep-rooted sin for us.

A spiritual revolution in America will take place when we walk in humility before God and each other. We will find ourselves in a place of receiving blessing from God when we have a contrite spirit. And we can expect revival throughout the land when the church is filled with those who tremble at His Word!

Prayer Points

- Humble yourself before the Lord in prayer this day.
- Recognize the great need you have to be one who trembles at the Word of God.
- Pray for another Great Awakening to sweep the nation as the Lord's people learn to humble themselves with a contrite spirit, and to tremble at the Word of the Lord.

My Prayer

Oh, Lord, forgive us for our arrogance. We humble ourselves before You today. Forgive us of any pride. Help us to walk in humility before You and others. May a contrite spirit mark our lives continually. Teach us what it means to tremble at Your Word. Revive Your people, Lord. May another Great Awakening come to this nation as we walk in humility and contriteness before You!

DAY FORTY

"Who knows but that you have come to royal position for such a time as this?" –Esther 4:14

The well-known story of Esther becoming queen at a crucial time in the history of the Jewish people has inspired many through the years. The Jews faced annihilation at the hands of their enemies. Esther would be putting her life in danger by speaking out, but her cousin Mordecai's words gave her the courage she needed. He appealed to the timing of her part in this drama, "for such a time as this."

I believe it is God's timing that you have prayed your way through this little book. Like Esther, we are living in perilous times in which our nation is under assault from foreign enemies, and from those within who have failed to understand the critical role of the Christian faith to the greatness of America. It is a situation that cannot simply be fixed by a new leader, new plan, or different strategy. We need the intervention of God!

God steps in when His people passionately ask Him to. The most important thing Christians can do for America is to pray. In these days of distress, the Lord is raising up a people who will intercede with faith and fervency! You are answering the call. Pray . . . for such a time as this!

Prayer Points

• Thank the Lord for His great gift of prayer.
• Pray for a clearer understanding of the days in which we live and how we should pray.
• Pray for a spirit of prayer to come over the church in America.

My Prayer

Father, I am so grateful that You hear when we call. For weeks now, we have been praying for our beloved nation. Thank You for calling us to prayer and showing us how to pray. Give us an understanding of the times in which we live and Your purposes for our nation. We want always to line up our prayers with Your desires. Would You pour out a spirit of prayer upon the church in America? Show us that we are indeed called to pray for our nation for such a time as this.

Get a **GREATER** CONNECTION . . .

. . . and a **15%** DISCOUNT

PRAYERCONNECT

To subscribe by mail, fill out this form, enclose a check made
out to Prayer Connect and mail to:

PRAYERCONNECT
P.O. Box 10667
Terre Haute, IN 47801

CODED PRICES: Digital–**$16.99**; Print–**$21.24**; CPLN–**$25.50**

Name: _____

Address: _____

City: _____ ST: _____ Zip: _____

Email: _____

(Canadian and International subscribers must subscribe online with code. Your pricing on Print or
CPLN is higher due to shipping costs.)

BKDCJS

GIVE A **GIFT SUBSCRIPTION**
TO A FRIEND

To subscribe by mail, fill out this form, enclose a check made
out to Prayer Connect and mail to:

PRAYERCONNECT
P.O. Box 10667
Terre Haute, IN 47801

CODED PRICES: Digital–**$16.99**; Print–**$21.24**; CPLN–**$25.50**

Name: _____

Address: _____

City: _____ ST: _____ Zip: _____

Email: _____

(Canadian and International subscribers must subscribe online with code. Your pricing on Print or
CPLN is higher due to shipping costs.)

BKDCJS